AF326591

ECHOES OF RESILIENCE

My Humble Beginnings in Africa and Giving Back to Africa

By
Sidiki Traoré

Cover Design by Lenjo Maza
Formatting by Lisa Grimes

ISBN: 978-1-62429-536-2

Published through
Opus Self-Publishing
Located at:
Politics & Prose Bookstore
5015 Connecticut Ave NW
Washington, D.C. 20008
www.politics-prose.com // (202) 364-1919

Acknowledgements

I wish to thank the following people:

I would like to extend my heartfelt gratitude to **Jean Claude Daddy Sekanyambo** for his invaluable contributions to this book. His suggestions, recommendations, and editing have been instrumental in shaping this narrative. I am deeply indebted to him.

I wish to thank **Judie Artman** for helping with the organization and editing of the book. Also, thanks to **Lisa Grimes**, our incredible designer for over 9 years and the talented **Lenjo Asad Maza** for designing all our cover pages as well for over 9 years.

Special thanks to all of the team members at the Darden School of Business of the University of Virginia (UVA) that have been supportive of the flagship program of Distance Education for Africa (DeAfrica), known as the "Africa Scholarship Cohort", namely **Dr. Joanne Meier, Dr. Katherine Beach, Kathryn Lynn Surchek, Dr. Kristin Palmer, and Michael Koenig,** who were there from the very beginning of the collaboration with Distance Education for Africa.

I also wish to thank my former boss from the World Bank, **Professor Peter Materu**, and **Professor Marito Garcia** for their help.

TABLE OF CONTENTS

PROLOGUE

The purpose of this book is to share the story of my journey from growing up in Mali, the reasons behind my departure to the U.S., and my educational path. It also details my efforts in giving back to Africa. My hope is that this book will inspire future generations to dream big, never give up on their dreams, and to always think of and to help others.

Success Story: Dawit Insurance Agency Limited
(Nairobi, Kenya)

Selam Bekele, born in Addis Ababa, Ethiopia, is a graduate of the United States International University in Kenya with a degree in Information Systems and Technology and a Master's in Business Administration with a concentration in Strategic Management. She is married to a Kenyan, Ken Kairu, and they have two daughters aged 14 and 11. She is also the founder of a non-profit organization, The Shrine from Within, and is a trained teacher, transformational and family success coach, author, and digital transformation and business strategy consultant.

Selam and Ken founded Dawit Insurance Agency Limited, and were able to transform their small family business through the African Scholarship Cohort (ASC) which was launched in 2016 by the Darden School of Business at the University of Virginia (UVA) in collaboration with Distance Education for Africa (DeAfrica). Selam took 14 DeAfrica courses with UVA, which significantly impacted her business's success.

As a result of the courses offered, they succeeded in: increasing their insurance sales, automating their insurance claim process, transforming their marketing strategies, and were able to develop a strategic plan for their company's future.

The UVA courses, particularly "Design Thinking", helped them view their business from a customer-centric perspective. They have won multiple awards in Kenya for excellence in the insurance industry.

Selam's is just one of many lives that have been touched by DeAfrica and the ASC; her and Ken's story, and the stories of so many like them, are the driving force behind my mission to give back to Africa and why I am writing this book to inspire others to be active in giving back to their communities. This book is not just my story, but the story of those who have helped me find my path and who continue to guide me in my mission.

PART I:

MY HUMBLE BEGINNINGS IN AFRICA

CHAPTER 1

OUELESSEBOUGOU TO BAMAKO

My Hometown: Ouelessebougou, the Republic of Mali

I am originally from Mali, a French West African colony that gained its independence in September 1960. I was born in the small village of Ouelessebougou, which has since grown into a small town. Situated in the Cercle de Kati in the Koulikoro Region of southwestern Mali, Ouelessebougou is located in a tropical area with a rainy season from May to October and a dry season—the local climate consists of these two main seasons. Ouelessebougou covers an area of approximately 1,118 square kilometers and includes 44 villages. According to the 2009 census, the commune had a population of 50,056. It is known for its rich historical background and is located only 80 kilometers south of Bamako, Mali's capital city.

Ouelessebougou was founded around 800 years ago by the Samaké family; two brothers, Ngolo and Oueressé, who discovered it while hunting near a small stream. The name "Oueressé" was transformed in French to "Ouelesse" and "*bougou*" means "village" in Bambara, forming Ouelesebougou. Upon its formation around 1748, the village had three major families: Diawara, Doumbia, and Soumahoro.

Even today, the predominant ethnic group in Oulessebougou is the Bambara, particularly the Samaké clan. Other ethnic groups include the Fulani, Samogo, Mossi (my father's ethnic group), Khorogho, and Sarakole.

Agriculture is the mainstay of the local economy of Ouelessebougou. The Bambara people are subsistence farmers, cultivating millet, maize, sorghum, rice, fonio, and peanuts. Traditional farming methods involve the use of small hoes and animal-drawn plows. Livestock raising, including sheep, goats, cattle, and donkeys, serves as a form of savings account, as there were no local banks.

Women engage in shea butter production and gardening, as well as selling vegetables in weekly markets.

Islam is the predominant religion in the area, with a minority adhering to Christianity. There is a Baptist church in an area called Ntentou, and the Mormon Church from Utah has created a city alliance with Ouelessebougou, contributing to local development.

A Glimpse into My Childhood and Family Life: A Life Without Modern Convenience

Growing up in a village without electricity or running water shared my childhood profoundly. We had a well in the middle of our compound, a group of houses surrounded by a wall. Pulling water from the well was a daily task, as it provided our household with drinking water.

Every evening, my father would send me to buy kerosene to fill the lamps in our home. Under the soft glow of these lamps, we would study and carry out our evening activities.

My Father and his Work Ethic: Musa Traoré

My father, Musa Traoré, was part of the Mossi ethnic group and was born in 1918 in Ouagadougou, the capital of Burkina Faso, formerly known as Upper Volta. In his thirties, my father moved to Mali, settling in the village of Dialakoroba, about 30 miles south of Bamako. He worked for a businessman named Nfaly Haidara, a table merchant selling various goods. My father would travel long distances on bicycle, carrying these goods to sell in weekly markets.

My father's hard work eventually led to him buying a bicycle for me— the first one in our village. It added a great source of pride for me and envy for the other children, who often asked to ride it. This bicycle became a symbol of success and was a significant marker of our improved circumstances.

After nine years of hard work, my father moved to Ouelessebougou and became a successful businessman known as "Mossi Moussa". Despite being illiterate, he had an incredible memory for business calculations and was highly respected in the community. His generosity and commitment to helping others left a lasting impression on me. He would bring food from his trips to share with the family and always found ways to be supportive of the community.

My father's dedication to his work was unmatched. Starting with a bicycle and later upgrading to a motorbike, he traveled to weekly markets in neighboring villages every day—except Tuesdays. The following was his travel schedule:

> **Monday** – *Keleya*
> **Tuesdays** – off
> **Wednesday** – *Sidoba*
> **Thursday** – *Bamako* (for new merchandise)
> **Friday** – *Ouelessebougou*
> **Saturday** – *Dialakoroba* or *Sélingué*
> **Sunday** – *Dingua*

My father's entrepreneurial spirit, hard work, and generosity have deeply influenced my own values and efforts to give back to Africa.

Family Dynamics and Marriages

My mother, Nana Traoré, married my father through an arranged marriage organized by his former boss, Mr. Nfaly Haidara, as a gesture of gratitude for my father's service. She was born in 1923 and passed away when I was very young. Although my memories of her are few, I remember her as often being sick. Family members later speculated that she might have died of breast cancer.

My father married a second wife while my mother was still alive. She bore him four children. After my mother's death, my stepmother continued to care for our blended family. Concerned about our family's welfare, my grandfather arranged for my mother's younger sister, Sitan, to marry my father. Sitan had already been a part of our household, helping my ailing mother. She married my father to ensure we were well cared for after my mother's passing, following the tradition in our society where a younger sister can marry her older sister's husband if the elder sister passes away.

When I was growing up, traditional marriages were the norm. Parents would often find wives for their sons, and, in many cases, the sons and daughters had little say in the matter—although in rare instances they could refuse. In Mali, men pay a dowry, or bride price, which is given to the wife and her family by the husband. This is not viewed as a sale or commercial transaction, but rather as a ceremonial tradition.

Another cultural tradition in Mali, and many parts of Africa, is polygamy, where a man can marry multiple wives if he has the financial means. In Islam, men are permitted to marry up to four wives.

There are many different forms of marriage in the world, including some that allow for the continuation of marital alliances after the death of a spouse:

Polygamy: a plural marriage that can be either 'polygyny' or polyandry. Polygyny is the marriage of a man to more than one woman at a time. Polyandry is when a woman takes more than one husband at a time; this can be found in Polynesia's Marue Islanders and among groups in Tibet, Nepal, and India.

Sororate: in many cases, a man may marry his deceased wife's sister to maintain his ties with her family. If an older sister passes away, the younger sister can marry the widower. This was the case with my aunt, Sitan, who married my father after my mother, her older sister, passed away.

Levirate: Similarly, in some traditions, a woman may marry her deceased husband's brother to maintain the family alliance. If an older brother dies, his younger brother can marry the wive(s). If the older brother had multiple wives, all of them may be married to the brothers in the family. This type of marriage may or may not involve sexual relations between parties.

I have a friend who was in a similar proposition after his older brother passed away. He felt that these practices were outdated and refused to marry one of his brother's widows. Instead, he moved out of the family home and settled with his only wife.

Serial Monogamy: having more than one spouse over time, but never more than one at a time.

My father's family were also present in my life; my Uncle Hamidou's devotion to my father, his older brother, was unwavering. He left Burkina Faso in search of my father, eventually reuniting with him in

Mali. Their bond was incredibly strong, characterized by shared values of honesty, dedication, and respect. Hamidou sacrificed his personal life to work for my father, showing a selflessness that deeply influenced our family.

Uncle Hamidou's first wife, Gala Fanta, was an extraordinary woman who had thirteen children, including a set of triplets. She managed a business selling *fari*, a labor-intensive local delicacy made of beans cooked with onions and blended with spices. Though the work was hard, her efforts helped support her family. My Uncle also had a second wife, Mah Djan, who had five children with him. It was an arranged marriage and, as she was much younger, their marriage ended in divorce due to generational differences and misunderstandings.

CHAPTER 2

CAPITAL EDUCATION: TRANSITION TO BAMAKO

After failing my secondary school exams, my father sent me to a private school in Mali's Capital city of Bamako for a year. He bought me a bicycle to use for the commute. My experience of carrying goods on a bicycle from my hometown to nearby village markets proved helpful for this commute. Some of my classmates were surprised by the distance I traveled daily, and I successfully commuted for the entire school year.

It was a challenging commute as I had to ride from the suburb of Sogoninko, then cross the Niger River bridge that divides Bamako, and then continue all the way downtown. The bridge crossing could be very dangerous. If a cyclist fell in the middle of the road, it often led to other accidents and significant traffic jams. The bridge did have a narrow lane for bicycles and mopeds; it was constructed like a sidewalk along the bridge. I managed this difficult commute on a bicycle, driven by my father's lesson that hard work always pays off. Whenever I thought about his advice, it gave me the motivation to push through each day.

With hard work, I passed the exams and was admitted to the Lycée de Badalabougou, a prestigious high school in Bamako. I was skinny and tall in high school and classmates gave me the nickname "Elegant Man" while I was in high school. I spent three years there; I still remember sometimes having to study under streetlights during power outages.

After high school, I pursued a BA in English at the Ecole Normale Supérieure in Bamako, taught by both British and American instructors. After graduating in 1979, I went on to be an instructor as well, teaching English at the Lycée Dougoukolo Konaré in Kayes for four years.

Seeking further education, I made the decision to move to Paris. There, I earned a Master's Degree in Linguistics and Language from the University of Paris VII.

My journey from a village with no modern amenities to teaching English and studying in Paris is a testament to resilience and the pursuit of education. The well in our compound, the kerosene lamps, and my father's bicycle are symbols of. a past that shaped my path, leading me to new opportunities and broader horizons.

The well of our compound and, in the background, the mud house where I was born.

My Father (left) and My Uncle Hamidou (right)

My father, Musa Traoré

My Uncle Hamidou and his first wife Gala Fanta

My aunt Sitan seated with my father

Gala Fanta cooking "fari"

Me, *"Elegant Man" in High School*

From left to right: Me, Emmanuel Edward, John House, Barema Niagando, and Ginny Wagner, friends from my teacher training college at the Ecole Nationale Supérieure (ENSup)

Classmates from the English Department 1975-1979 at Ecole Normale Supérieure du Mali

PART II:

GLOBAL EDUCATION – FROM PARIS, FRANCE TO BLOOMINGTON, INDIANA

CHAPTER 3

CULTURE SHOCK: NAVIGATING A NEW LIFE ABROAD

During my time in Paris, I was enrolled in a master's degree program at the University of Paris VII. Alongside my studies there, I also took courses at the Institut National des Langues et Civilizations Orientales (INALCO). INALCO is a French university specializing in the teaching of languages and cultures from around the world, including those of Central Europe, Africa, Asia, America, and Oceania.

At INALCO, I studied under Professor Gérard Dumestre, a Frenchman who taught Bambara, my native language. While it might seem surprising to some that a Frenchman was teaching me my own language, Professor Dumestre was instrumental in deepening my understanding of Bambrara's structure, grammar, syntax, and parts of speech—things that native speakers often overlook. His pedagogy prepared me to teach Bambara effectively.

My time at INALCO was pivotal in my academic journey. It not only solidified my linguistic skills, but also opened doors for my future. It was at INALCO that I met an American missionary who was also learning Bambara. He encouraged me to apply to Indiana University (IU), which marked the beginning of my journey to the United States.

The United States: Indiana University in Bloomington

The opportunity to teach and study at IU significantly advanced my academic and professional career. Indiana University (IU) offered me the position of Assistant Teacher (AT) in the Linguistics Department. And so I began my journey to the United States. Going to Indiana University required adjusting to a new culture, society, and educational system that significantly shaped my life in the West.

I initially knew very little about Bloomington, Indiana. I arrived in Bloomington by flying from New York to Indianapolis, where a driver picked me up and we took the 50-mile drive to Bloomington.

Bloomington is a moderately small town in America, home to Indiana University which has just over 45,000 students. It is renowned for its "Hoosiers", a term used for natives of Indiana, and its strong basketball culture. When I arrived in 1985, the basketball team had just won the US Championship and a big, wild celebration took place.

In addition to sports, the University is famous for its music school and its African Studies Department, which hired me to teach Bambara while also providing a fee remission that enabled me to study and teach simultaneously. This support was crucial in allowing me to pursue and complete my academic goals; in my six years at IU, I earned two master's degrees: an MS in Instructional Systems Technology and an MA in Applied Linguistics.

When I first arrived in Bloomington, I initially stayed at Eigeman Hall, a dormitory with a cafeteria. The dorm was nice and hosted many international students from around the world. The cafeteria offered diverse foods—the rice bowls were particularly popular among Asian and African students.

After one semester, I decided to move out of the dorms and into single housing that was owned by the university. When I arrived in Bloomington, I didn't know how to cook. This was a huge cultural difference from Mali, where traditional gender roles in our culture meant men didn't cook. A friend from Mali, Lajdi Sacko, taught me how to cook before I moved out. Lajdi taught me various dishes, including peanut butter chicken sauce and rice. I was surprised to see that most African men on campus knew how to cook. I ended up loving cooking and even learned to prepare dishes like "Thieboudienne" from Senegal and "Ugali" from Kenya. When I told my parents back home that I could cook, they didn't believe it.

My first day in linguistics class was quite a shock. The professor handed out the syllabus and started the course immediately. American students actively participated, asking questions, debating, and even challenging the professor—something I wasn't used to from my experiences in France and Africa. Foreign students generally sat quietly and took notes.

Some other cultural differences that struck me were:

- Office Hours. American Professors are very accessible to students and have office hours for student appointments. This level of interaction was very new to me.

- Social Clubs. Fraternities and Sororities were cultural elements that I hadn't encountered in France or Africa but that are an important part of the American college experience.

- Visiting the Homes of Professors. Dr. Charles Bird, one of the linguistics professors, organized large parties featuring African and American music. Another professor from the Department of Instructional Systems Technology invited me to his home, showing me a room full of toys for his daughter. This excess made me reflect on the disparities between Africa and the US; after this experience I was inspired to think about how I could help underprivileged kids in Africa.

- Typing Term Papers. One of the biggest challenges for me and for other African students was typing term papers. Growing up in Africa, typewriters were rare, and only secretaries knew how to type. I learned about a Canadian woman from Alberta, then in her seventies, who charged African students to type their term papers. She typed all my papers for me, providing a crucial service.

As a Teaching Assistant (TA) at the University for Bambara courses, I taught students from various departments, including Criminal Justice, Anthropology, Ethnology, and Linguistics.

They took my class for various reasons; some for their foreign language requirements, some for research, others as an elective. I initially wore a suit and tie to my first class, but after a professor's comment about having a "hot date", I realized the casual dress code on campus and adjusted accordingly.

The African Students' Association in Bloomington was vibrant and active, organizing many events: volleyball competitions, soccer matches, fashion shows, and something called Africa Day which featured foods from many African countries. These activities allowed me to meet people from different parts of Africa and to learn about many cultures and traditions.

In addition to these Africa Days, the African Students Association organized student protests against South Africa. Disinvestment (or divestment) from South Africa was first advocated in the 1960s as a protest against the country's apartheid regime. When I arrived in Bloomington in 1985, there was a significant student movement across U.S. universities, urging their administrations to divest from South Africa and its regime. Anti-apartheid activists throughout the U.S. encouraged students to protest on their campuses and the African Students Association was particularly active on this front.

There were other opportunities to educate American students on African life and culture. I had a friend, Marc, who taught at a high school in Mitchell, Indiana, a small city with a population of just over 4,000 in Marion Township in Lawrence County. Mitchell was not far from Bloomington where I lived. Marc often invited me to his school to speak to his students about Africa.

Many would mention negative stereotypes such as disease, famine, and poverty. I would show them postcards of cities like Abidjan in Côte d'Ivoire, Nairobi in Kenya, and Harare in Zimbabwe—they were always surprised to see skyscrapers in Africa. Then, I would turn the table, and list some stereotypes some Africans have about America: a very wealthy country where people drive limousines and fancy cars, like those seen in TV shows such as *Dallas* or *Dynasty*; people living in skyscrapers and having over a million dollars in their bank accounts; owning five to ten cars. The students would laugh and tell me that no one in their class was that rich.

I would go on to explain that images and television can sometimes create false impressions of a country or continent. For example, if people constantly see images of the homelessness in U.S. cities, they might believe that many Americans are homeless or poor. It's an important reminder of how media can distort our perceptions of different places.

I also learned new things about American culture. I remember once an American man I met told me he had gone camping alone. This was surprising to me as the concept of being alone was unusual in my village where collectivism and solidarity were the norm. In my community back home, men would work together on farms, attend funerals together, and share goods, emphasizing the importance of mutual support and togetherness. The experiences in Bloomington exposed me to new ideas and inspired me to contribute to the betterment of Africa.

After my tenure at IU, I moved to Washington DC and spent six years teaching French at the Foreign Service Institute (FSI). There, my students included Ambassadors, Foreign Service Officers, Defense Attachés, and other government officials. This experience broadened my teaching expertise and reinforced my commitment to and passion for language education.

My educational journey from Paris to Indiana University significantly shaped my professional trajectory, enabling me to contribute to distance education initiatives like the African Virtual University. The AVU's mission to improve access to education in Africa aligns with my passion for leveraging technology to bridge educational gaps and empower future generations.

Me at the Student Services Building of Indiana University

Me (in red) at an Apartheid Protest in Bloomington

Additional images of protests in Bloomington

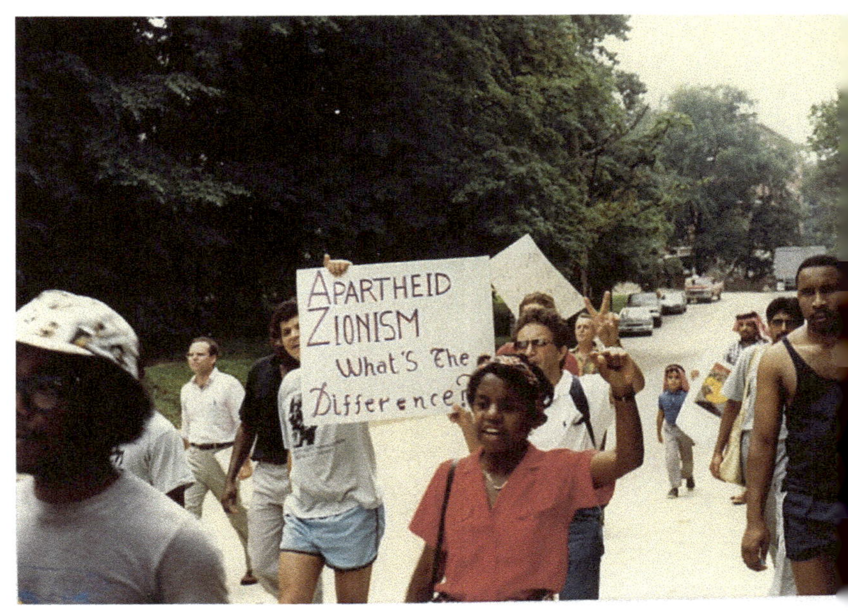

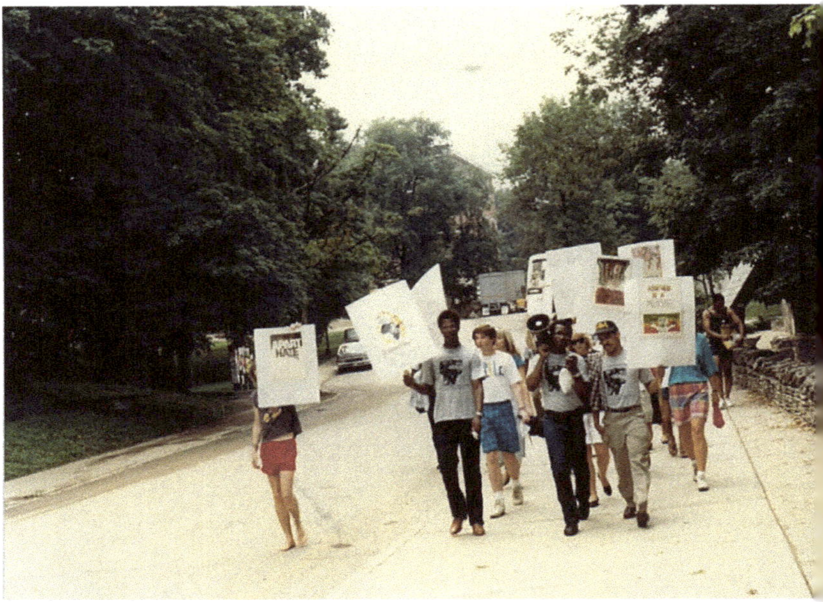

Chapter 4

AFRICAN VIRTUAL UNIVERSITY: AN OVERVIEW

In 1995, the World Bank initiated the African Virtual University, a satellite-based distance education project designed to deliver university education in the disciplines of science and engineering, providing non-credit continuing education programs and remedial instruction to Sub-Saharan Africa (SSA). Preparatory work for the pilot phase began in September 1995 and it received funding from the Africa Region and INFODEV programs.

It was founded by Etienne Baranshamaje, a visionary Burundian national. The project began in a modest studio within the World Bank Office, where Baranshamaje was assisted by Khadidiatou Sene, a dedicated Language Program Assistant from Senegal.

The objectives of AVU:

- To train a large number of African scientists, technicians, engineers, business managers, and employees.

- To encourage the further development of newly educated professionals.

- To provide an academic environment for African educational institutions, faculty, and students to participate in the global learning community.

The Key Developments of African Virtual University (1997 – 2003)

1997/1998

- The World Bank approved grants for six Anglophone countries in Africa to set up Learning Centers: Zimbabwe, Tanzania, Uganda, Ethiopia, Kenya, and Ghana.

- Courses in science, mathematics, and technology were broadcasted from institutions in the United States and Ireland.

1999

- AVU expanded to offer computer science courses from institutions like the Université Libre de Bruxelles in Belgium and the Université Laval in Canada.

2000

- Over 24,000 students register for semester-long courses.

- AVU establishes itself as a legally independent organization with a network of 26 Learning Centers in 15 SSA countries.

- In February 2000, AVU International (AVUi) is established as a non-profit NGO in Washington DC. For legal reasons, two separate non-profit organizations (NPOs) were set up; one in Nairobi, Kenya (African Virtual University-AVU) and the other in Washington DC (AVU International-AVUi). AVU and AVUi are separate organizations and are governed by separate articles of incorporation and bylaws.

2001

- AVU transitions core operations from Washington DC to Nairobi.

- Accenture conducts a strategic review, recommending AVU reposition itself as an education network architect and integrator.

- On July 30, 2001, the AVU Board of Directors hold a meeting in Nairobi, Kenya.

- The Java Revolution Course in collaboration with the Massachusetts Institute of Technology (MIT) is launched. 178 students from 13 Learning Centers Universities participated in the Programs.

2002

- AVU becomes an intergovernmental organization based in Nairobi, Kenya.

- The Vice Chancellors Conference in Nairobi approved transferring key operations to Nairobi.

2003/2004

- The Francophone Computer Science Degree program launches with multiple universities.

- There is a shift in focus from brokered foreign content to developing programs in conjunction with. African partner institutions.

- By 2003 the staff has grown to a larger multinational and multiracial staff—many Kenyans, and Canadian, French, British, Australian, American, Senegalese, Tanzanian, Burundian, Nigerian, Malian, Ugandan, Burkinabe.

The AVU Partnership and Consolidation Project and Subsequent Developments

The ATICS Initiative was launched in 2004, surveying eighty-three universities across Africa, creating a database on ICT and connectivity information. More information can be found at www.antics.info . This project was contracted by the Partnership for Higher Education in Africa with support from the World Bank.

BANDWIDTH CONSORTIUM

- **Consortium Formation**: This enabled 10 African universities, the Association of African Universities, and the Kenya Educational Network of thirty-three tertiary institutions to purchase bandwidth.
- **Funding**: Provided by the Partnership for Higher Education in Africa (Ford, Rockefeller, McArthur, Carnegie, and Hewlett Foundations).
- **Objective**: Switch network to Intelsat in February 2006 at an estimated cost of $2.33 per kilobyte, per second, per month.

INSTITUTIONAL DEVELOPMENTS

- **Departments and Facilities:**
  - Creation of the Department of Instructional Technology and Design (later Open Distance and Electronic Learning (ODeL)) under Peter Bateman.
  - Establishment of the Research and Innovation Facility (RIF) to support eLearning research.
- **Licensing Agreements**: Renegotiation with institutions like RMIT, University of Curtin, and Laval.
- **Committees**: Formation of Academic and Technology, Finance, Human Resources, and Curriculum Coordination Committees. The Curriculum Coordination Committee held its inaugural workshop in October 2004.
- **Regional Office:** Decision to open a regional office in Dakar, Senegal.

PROJECTS AND COLLABORATIONS

- **Teacher Education Project**: This project was approved by the African Development Bank with a $7.5 million grant and was done in collaboration with MIT OpenCourseWare for access to educational content at Addis Ababa University and the University of Nairobi. Participating countries: Djibouti, Ethiopia, Kenya, Madagascar, Mozambique, Somalia, Tanzania, Uganda, Zambia, and Zimbabwe.
- **Workshops**: The first workshops on teacher training were held in Nairobi (May) and then in Madagascar (November).
- **Graduation**: The first ever graduation ceremony of the program took place in 2005 with fifty-two anglophone and thirty francophone students.

CHALLENGES AND TRANSITIONS

- **Leadership Changes:** There were several key resignations in 2006, including Peter Bateman (Manager of ODeL), Derick Pierson (CFO), and Bolaji Akinboro (Project Manager). Peter Kuzvinesta Dzvimbo resigned a year later in 2007, with Dr. Bakary Diallo becoming Acting Rector.
- **Status Change:** NGO status was cancelled, though AVU retained its status as an Inter-Governmental Organization (IGO).
- **Funding**: The Hewlett Foundation announced a grant for the RIF project in 2006.

AVU PROGRAMS AND INITIATIVES

- **Learning Centers**: Fifty-three centers across 28 countries.
- **Degree and Diploma Programs:**
  - Business Administration – offered by Curtin University in Ethiopia, Kenya, Tanzania, and Rwanda
  - Computer Science – offered in English by RMIT in Kenya, Ethiopia, Ghana, Rwanda, Tanzania, and Namibia. Offered in French by Université Laval in Senegal, Benin, Niger, Mauritania, and Burundi.

- **Short Professional and Continuing Education (SPaCE) Program:** Offering programs in Computer Science, Journalism, Information Technology, and Business Communication.
- **Teacher Education and Training Program:** Focuses on ICT application in Mathematics and Science Education.
- **Open Distance and eLearning (ODeL) Initiative:**
  - Capacity Building – through the Capacity Enhancement Program (ACEP) which aimed at enhancing ODeL capabilities.
  - Research and Innovation Facility (RIF) – supported basic and applied research in ODeL.

The African Virtual University Team in 2003
I am standing on the far right (in blue)

Java Revolution students from the University of Zimbabwe in Harare

*The African Virtual University Team, clockwise, from top left:
Bruno Donat (Business Development); Bruno Donat with Prof. Peter Materu
(Executive Interim CEO); Danielle Savard (Francophone Program Officer): Mike
Kessler (Manager, Business and Technology Channel); Michelle Jackson
(Administrative Assistant); Shola Aboderin (AVU World Bank Liaison); Alex
Twinomughisha (Technical Coordinator) with Pamela Arrey (Financial Officer) and
Musa Sall (Studio Technician); Me (Site Liaison Officer)*

*The AVU Board of Directors Meeting in Nairobi, Kenya on July 30, 2001.
Standing, left to right: Bruno Donat, David Potten, Peter Materu, Magdallen Juma,
Alan Williams, Ted Ahlers, Dwight Hutchins, Shola Aboderin, Philip Regan, Bolaji
Akinboro, Alex Twinomugisha. Seated, left to right: François Rajaoson, John
Middleton, Pinias Makhurane, Sam Adjepong, Lionel Baldwin, Soumana Sako*

Etienne Barajamashe, founder of the African Virtual University

CHAPTER 5

MY CULTURAL EXPERIENCES GAINED FROM TRAVEL IN AFRICA WITH AVU

During my tenure with the African Virtual University, I traveled extensively across the African continent, immersing myself in diverse cultures. Many of the beliefs and traditional practices I encountered were profoundly fascinating. There are two cultural elements that I witnessed and experienced in Somaliland and Senegal that truly impacted me.

Value Systems and the Meaning of Trust in Somali Society

According to *The Economist*, the clan system is very strong in Somalia and has fostered a deep sense of community and trust among the Somali people.

Somalis are a homogenous people with a strong sense of identity, culturally aligned with the Middle East. They have a robust Somali-Islamic culture that influences every aspect of life—social, economic, and political—all framed by cultural values that emphasize strong social capital built on trust. For instance, Dahabshill, Africa's largest money transfer business—operating in 126 countries—is described by *The Economist* as a money-transfer firm with big ambitions. In Somalia, a customer can be handed over $200,000 in cash, and no one would touch or rob that person. These trust values significantly discourage theft and bank robbery.

I recall some incredible beliefs and traditions in Somalia/Somaliland. On a mission to Hargeisa, the capital city of Somaliland, I needed to exchange some US dollars for the local currency. I was informed that there was no formal bureau de change. Instead, I was led to a local open-air market to exchange my US dollars with local "money changers", individuals specialized in converting foreign currencies to local Somali currency. To my astonishment, I saw piles of money stacked on the ground, waiting for customers. The level of trust within the community was truly remarkable. Money is traded here in brick-size bundles and customers take the local currency home in bags they bring themselves.

My trip to Hargeisa was eye-opening because I had never seen or heard anything like it in my life. When I left the capital city, I showed pictures like the ones below to many friends and colleagues who remarked that in most other places, leaving money out in the open like that would invite theft and violence. However, in Somali tradition, such acts are simply not committed. Despite hearing many negative things about money, the money exchangers remain unrobbed, a testament to the unique cultural values and trust within the Somali community.

Noise Pollution in Africa

Having lived in the United States for a long time, I became accustomed to respecting noise pollution regulations and keeping music at a low volume. However, in parts of Africa, such as Gambia, Mali, Senegal, and Mauritania, noise pollution seems like a Western concept. In Nairobi, I often got headaches from riding in "matatus" (public buses) where the music was so loud it made my entire body vibrate.

Nancy Duncan, an American who travelled to Senegal remarked that in West Africa, particularly in Senegal, finding a quiet space to read privately can sometimes be difficult. In Africa, communal living from the cradle to the grave is the norm; the desire for solitude and quietness can be seen as strange. However, globalization may be bringing changes to these traditions.

Nancy also said that in Africa, background noise is an integral part of daily life and often goes unnoticed. The concept of "noise pollution" is distinctly Western.

In Africa, noise signifies togetherness and helps to combat loneliness. For example, the *goorgoorlu*, or the hustle to make a daily living, can be seen in all parts of Senegal, especially the markets in Dakar such as Colobane, Tilien, HLM, and Gueuele Tapée. Around one o'clock in the afternoon the Sandaga market in downtown Dakar is full of many sounds: cars breaking, honking, people loudly asking for donations (a practice known as *maajaal* done by religious disciples of Baye Fall), "*wanter wanter*" ("sale sale") by merchants trying to attract customers with dances and drumming–all of these create a lively bustling atmosphere.

While I was living in Dakar, I started making a list of the noises around me. This list might also be of interest to and fascinate Westerners as it highlights the constant assault on the eardrums from various sources—human, machine, and animal.

Here is the list I kept:

Religious
- *Public Prayers – loud music and chanting, often continue until late at night, with streets blocked by religious leaders;*
- *Songs – men singing religious songs throughout the night;*
- *"Muezzin" –calls to prayer from loudspeakers five times a day, with the "muezzin" acting as the human church bell;*
- *Recorded verses – Arabic verses blaring from mosque loudspeakers all day long;*
- *Baye Fal – followers of the Baye Fall muslim sect in Sengegal;*
- *"Talibe" – begging children seeking alms;*

Nature
- *Ocean noise – the sound of waves in Dakar*

Animals
- *Goats and sheep – bleating from neighboring houses*
- *House Sheep – bleating from sheep kept within homes;*
- *Horses – used for work and transport;*
- *Stray dogs – barking, especially when in heat;*
- *Roosters – crowing, often at dawn;*

Cooking
- *Pots – the sound of pots rattling and clattering, lids being dropped to the ground;*
- *Mortars –house girls and maids pounding ingredients;*
- *Water – the sound of water running and buckets being filled*

Machines & Vehicles

- *Car repairs – mechanics working on vehicles;*
- *Welders – metal workers using power tools;*
- *Car doors – slamming as cars come and go;*
- *Vehicles – various types of cars and trucks;*
- *Mopeds – zipping through the streets;*
- *Public buses – "transports en commun" navigating the city;*
- *Taxi drivers – aggressively honking to attract customers;*
- *Airplanes – taking off and landing at Dakar airport;*
- *Generators – running constantly to combat frequent power outages;*

Music & Entertainment

- *All-Night parties – rooftop parties with loudspeakers;*
- *Street vendors – blasting music to attract attention and customers at Sandaga market;*
- *TV Programs – soap operas, news bulletins, music programs, and sports broadcasts;*

Trash Collection

- *Trash trucks – loud horns from both government trash trucks;*
- *Private trash collectors – wheelbarrows and carts with beeping horns, knocking on doors;*
- *Horse-drawn carts – trash collectors using horse-drawn carts for collection;*

Vendors

- *Street Peddlers – craftsmen and odd-jobbers making noise with their tools;*
- *Pedicurists on the fly – snapping and clicking scissors to attract customers;*
- *Beggars – walking with bowls, seeking alms*
- *Music vendors – selling CDs and cassettes with blaring boom boxes;*
- *Firecracker vendors – selling firecrackers*
- *Peanut sellers – women selling fresh peanuts in bowls balanced on their heads;*
- *Ice Cream vendors – loudly announcing their presence;*
- *Broom sellers – calling out "balai" as they walk through the neighborhoods;*
- *Fruit sellers – selling from horse-carts and wheelbarrows;*
- *Women fish sellers – carrying containers of fish on their heads;*
- *Cart vendors – selling small fish from their carts;*
- *Large fish sellers – offering fish like thiof, dorade, and yaor;*

Daily Life

- *Children – playing and screaming;*
- *Radios – small portable radios tuned to "Radio France Internationale";*
- *Construction – noise from masons working on houses;*
- *Advertisements – loudspeakers on cars for commercials and political rallies;*

Departure from African Virtual University

In 2010, upon my departure from AVU, I left with a wealth of skills and knowledge that I honed during my tenure; I was ready to embark on a new journey. Equipped with the experience and expertise gained at AVU, I felt prepared to establish an organization aimed at facilitating access to quality education for Africans, including those without means. The foundation laid by AVU served as the bedrock upon which Distance Education for Africa (DeAfrica) was built, enabling me to pursue my vision with confidence and determination.

PART III:

DISTANCE EDUCATION FOR AFRICA

CHAPTER 6

DISTANCE EDUCATION FOR AFRICA

Distance Education for Africa (DeAfrica) is a nonprofit educational organization registered as a Charity in Washington DC, USA, and as a Non-Governmental Organization (NGO) in Nairobi, Kenya. Founded in 2010, DeAfrica specializes in scalable distance learning across Africa, leveraging e-learning platforms to provide accessible education.

In collaboration with the Darden Business School at the University of Virginia, USA, DeAfrica offers free workforce education and community support to reskill and upskill Africans, aiming to create sustainable economic impact and advance gender equity through education. By extending quality education to individuals regardless of background, DeAfrica ensures that online courses, complemented by local mentors, reach both urban and rural populations.

The flagship program of DeAfrica, the African Scholarship Cohort (ASC), has awarded over 60,000 scholarships, enabling learners from every African country to access courses at no cost.

This initiative aligns with the United Nations Sustainable Development Goals, particularly Goals 4 (Quality Education), 5 (Gender Equality), 8 (Decent Work and Economic Growth), and 10 (Reduced Inequalities).

Reasons for Enrolling in DeAfrica Courses

1. **Skill Deficiency at Local Institutions:**

   - Some students find that their local universities or institutions do not offer the specific skills they need. For example, students from the University of Bangui in the Central African Republic benefitted from courses offered by the University of Laval in computer science.

2. **Professional Development Needs**:

   - Lack of opportunities for professional development in their current jobs.

   - Relevance of courses to their profession.

   - Desire for career advancement and self-development.

   - Need for a balanced skill set for entrepreneurship.

   - Inability to manage multitasking required at work and in business.

3. **Busy Working Professionals**:

   - Online options are preferred due to busy schedules.

   - Flexibility in timing and pace of learning.

   - Avoidance of traffic congestion.

4. **Quality of Local Professional Development Courses**:

   - Local courses may not always be current or updated.

   - DeAfrica's online courses are practical, applicable to the job market, and aligned with new trends.

   - Offer career advancement opportunities.

   - Unique methodology including micro-learning, continuous education, and multisensory delivery methods.

- Provision of certificates for professional recognition on platforms like LinkedIn.

5.   **Low Morale and Budget Constraints**:

- Challenges such as low staff morale, limited resources in agencies or ministries, and poor working conditions.

- DeAfrica courses motivate staff and improve performance, despite budget constraints.

6.   **Lack of Training Budget in Government Agencies**:

- Many government agencies lack a training budget.

- DeAfrica courses provide an opportunity for staff to receive essential training, especially in areas like project planning and management.

7.   **Financial Constraints for African Students**:

- DeAfrica's free courses provide a lifeline for students facing financial constraints.

- Scholarships offered by DeAfrica represent an opportunity for unemployed individuals to access education that they couldn't afford otherwise.

8.   **Intellectual & Operational Assets for Senior Professionals**:

- Courses like Design Thinking are seen as valuable assets for senior professionals in roles such as education experts, offering intellectual and operational benefits for their work.

CHAPTER 7

THE DAWN OF DEAFRICA: PIONEERING EDUCATION ACCESS IN AFRICA

The inception of DeAfrica posed formidable challenges, marking the outset of a journey fraught with obstacles.

Established with an unwavering dedication to advancing education, DeAfrica has emerged as a trailblazer in pioneering innovative approaches to delivering high-quality, accessible, and impactful learning experiences throughout Africa. Our core principles are deeply rooted in the belief that education serves as a powerful catalyst for positive change, capable of transforming individuals and entire communities.

In our relentless pursuit of this mission, DeAfrica strategically forged a transformative partnership with Maestro, LLC, a distinguished education services provider. This collaboration marked the genesis of our English language programs, meticulously crafted to cater to the diverse needs of students and professionals across the African continent. Spearheading this initiative is Cara Fulton, a highly respected English teacher with a distinguished background in academia, including tenures at Howard University and presently at Johns Hopkins University's School of Advanced International Studies (SAIS).

At the heart of DeAfrica's commitment to leveraging technology for educational advancement is the visionary leadership of Sidiki Traore, the President, and Founder of the organization. Sidiki embarked on an extensive journey across West Africa (Mali, Senegal, Guinea, and Guinea-Bissau), Central Africa (the Democratic Republic of Congo and Central African Republic), and East Africa (South Sudan and

Kenya). His primary objective was to introduce and advocate for the transformative use of e-books in English language education.

During visits to 10 universities, it became evident that none were utilizing, or even aware of, the transformative potential of e-books for English language education. Undeterred, DeAfrica pioneered the adoption of e-books as a fundamental component of its Academic English Language program. This groundbreaking approach, led by Cara Fulton, allowed students to immerse themselves in interactive digital textbooks, complete with annotations from Prof. Fulton, transcending geographical barriers and reshaping the educational landscape.

DeAfrica's commitment to innovation extends beyond students to educators. Recognizing the need for comprehensive adoption, DeAfrica initiated a pioneering program to train English lecturers from esteemed institutions such as Kenyatta University. The focus was on equipping educators with the necessary skills to effectively utilize the Blackboard platform for teaching, eliminating the need for cumbersome commutes to satellite locations. This strategic endeavor not only saved valuable time and resources but also positioned these educators at the vanguard of modern pedagogical practices.

As we continue to evolve, DeAfrica remains steadfast as a beacon of transformative education, empowering individuals, and communities towards a future brimming with boundless possibilities. Through strategic partnerships, innovative educational programs, and an unwavering commitment to leveraging technology, DeAfrica is dedicated to leaving an indelible impact on the educational landscape of Africa.

Challenges and Attempts: The Beginning of DeAfrica

The inception of DeAfrica was marked by significant challenges, with the initial setup proving to be particularly demanding. In 2010, I ventured to Kenya to lay the groundwork for Distance Education for Africa. Amidst the trials and tribulations of those early days in Nairobi, perseverance became our guiding principle.

I started with a small team in Nairobi:

Lenjo Asad Maza, Communications Director and Graphic Designer
Maza was the backbone from the start. He assisted with all the necessary tools, marketing materials, legal documents, and provided a small office at Coxen House, across from the General Post Office in Nairobi. He designed marketing materials, which I distributed, even taking them to the airport to be carried by passengers to Burundi, the Democratic Republic of Congo, Mali, and Senegal.

Marcella Magara, Administration and Finance
Marcella managed our administration matters and the registration process.

John Kyalo, IT Specialist
John helped set up social media and provided tech support to learners facing connection issues and challenges.

Dr. Kristin Palmer, Online Director of the University of Virginia
Dr. Palmer joined when our collaboration with UVA started. She has worked tirelessly with the Africa Scholarship Cohort (ASC), interacting with learners from all over Africa. After Dr. Palmer's tenure with the UVA, she joined our team as DeAfrica's Director of Programs

As the Founder and President of DeAfrica, I couldn't have accomplished this without the incredible team mentioned above.

Our journey commenced with English courses, leveraging e-books to bridge the gap with French-speaking countries. Gradually expanding our offerings, we introduced journalism courses and teacher training programs. Additionally, collaborations with esteemed institutions like the University of Laval in Canada enriched our curriculum, bringing forth computer science courses of high caliber. Notably, cyber security courses, a cornerstone of modern education, were expertly delivered by a professor from the University of Maryland College Park, USA, further enhancing the breadth and depth of our educational initiatives.

CHAPTER 8

DeAfica's Achievements

Short Professional Development Courses
(2011-2015)

Over 10,000 professionals and students benefitted from our array of course offerings. These included:

- **English Language**, *Prof. Cara Fulton (Howard University)*
- **Academic English**, *Prof. Cara Fulton (Howard University)*
- **Using Online in Classroom**, *Prof. Cara Fulton (Howard University)*
- **Teacher Training, Using ICT in the Classroom**, *Prof. Cara Fulton*
- **Cyber Security,** *Prof. Rose Shumba (University of Maryland College Park)*
- **Global Challenges and International Relations**, *Prof. Fumiko Sasaki (Columbia University)*
- **Mass Media Communications and Journalism,** *Prof. Stanford Mukassa (Indiana University of Pennsylvania)*
- **Computer Security, Web Design, and Networking**, *University of Laval in Canada*
- **American History**, *Judie Artman (Montgomery Public Schools, Maryland)*
- **Introduction to Chinese,** *by Kuo Li (Confucius Institute, New Jersey City University)*
- **Sites Internet Dynamiques 1**
- **Programmation de base en Java**
- **Programmation en Visual Basic.net**
- **Réseaux sans fil**
- **Gestion de réseaux**

Africa Scholarship Cohort (ASC)
(2016-present)

The African Scholarship Cohort (ASC) is an innovative program that offers quality courses from prestigious institutions like the

University of Virginia and the University of London. Through its 60,000 scholarships, the cohort reaches learners across all African nations, creating the largest learning ecosystem on the continent. This initiative is built on the Community of Inquiry (CoI) framework, which has proven effective in online learning by fostering cognitive, teaching, and social presence.

The program also boasts a network of 100 regional mentors who provide essential training, motivation, advice, support, and coaching to students. By engaging in courses that cover topics such as Digital Transformation, Design Thinking for Innovation, Customer-Centric IT Strategies, and Project Management, participants gain valuable skills. These skills have empowered graduates to secure roles as Business Strategists, International Consultants, Innovation Specialists, and Business Development Specialists. The cohort has celebrated its achievements with 24 graduation ceremonies across the African continent and has published nine books that highlight student testimonials and document these events with photos.

In a 2023 survey, students of the ASC reported the following:

- 70% started new businesses
- 100% feel their skills have improved
- 15% received raises
- 95% reported a positive overall impact on their professional lives

Publications and Awards

I have co-authored multiple books along with Dr. Palmer and Maza. These have been great achievements that DeAfrica has made. I was the driving force behind these publications hence they are part of my autobiography. We have published four main books as well as a series of five Business Case Study Handbooks which feature over fifty case studies written by program participants, using analysis tools like Porter's Five Forces Analysis, Environmental Analysis, the 4Ps, the 4As, and SWOT Analysis.

DeAfrica's Graduation Ceremonies

Of all our achievements, one stands out the most: DeAfrica's graduation ceremonies stand as poignant milestones, brimming with profound emotions that underscore the transformative power of education. Witnessing the students express their gratitude and admiration, often accompanied by tears, serves as a testament to the impact of the organization's endeavors on individuals and communities across Africa.

Among the numerous graduations that have been held, two hold a special place in my heart. The inaugural ceremony took place at the University of Bangui in the Central African Republic in 2012, marking a significant milestone for DeAfrica. During this event, the weekly interactive sessions were broadcasted live through "Interwise," Laval University's delivery platform. This synchronous platform facilitated e-learning, collaboration, and communication, offering a unique blend of live, recorded, and self-paced learning experiences.

Ten students from the University of Bangui were enrolled in a Certificate Program on Computer Networking and Web Design, offered by Laval University in Quebec, Canada. Upon completion, they emerged equipped with skills that were previously scarce in their respective countries. Remarkably, some students secured employment with telecommunication companies even before completing the program, highlighting the tangible impact of their newfound expertise on their professional trajectories and the broader landscape of education in Africa.

Despite facing formidable challenges, the students in the Central African Republic (CAR) demonstrated unwavering determination and resilience throughout their educational journey with DeAfrica. One particularly striking example was a student who possessed only an old laptop, which he brought to campus for the live sessions. Despite the limited resources and poor internet connection, the students would gather around the laptop, eagerly participating in the sessions and diligently taking notes. The unreliable internet connection often interrupted the live sessions, causing disruptions and setbacks. However, these obstacles did not deter the students from their pursuit of knowledge. Instead, they persevered through the challenges, exhibiting remarkable resilience in the face of adversity. Their commitment to their education, despite the harsh conditions, serves as a testament to their unwavering determination and dedication to improving their futures through learning.

The second memorable graduation ceremony took place in Akobo, a remote and isolated village nestled in South Sudan, ten years later in the year 2022. The significance of this event cannot be overstated, as it symbolized the triumph of education over adversity in one of the most challenging environments imaginable.

In Akobo, access to education and resources is severely limited, with infrastructure and connectivity challenges hindering the pursuit of learning. Despite these formidable barriers, the community's commitment to education remained steadfast.

Against this backdrop, the graduation ceremony held profound significance. It represented not only the academic achievements of the students but also the resilience of the human spirit in the face of hardship. Families, friends, and community members gathered to celebrate the graduates, recognizing their perseverance and determination to overcome obstacles in pursuit of knowledge and brighter future.

The ceremony in Akobo served as a beacon of hope, inspiring others in the community to believe in the transformative power of education and to strive for excellence despite the odds. It was a testament to the indomitable human spirit and the profound impact that education can have on individuals and communities, even in the most challenging circumstances.

Embarking from the bustling capital of South Sudan, Juba, my journey to the remote village of Akobo was nothing short of extraordinary. With the aid of a United Nations' helicopter, I traversed vast distances, crossing rugged terrain and soaring over breathtaking landscapes to reach this isolated enclave.

Nestled amidst the untamed wilderness, Akobo stood as a testament to resilience in the face of adversity. Here, the Norwegian Refugee Council (NRC) had erected a beacon of hope: the Akobo Youth Center. Equipped with modest resources including a handful of computers and an internet connection, this center served as a lifeline for the village's youth.

Yet, the challenges facing Akobo were manifold. Intercommunal conflicts, fueled by longstanding grievances, cast a shadow over the community. Revenge killings and political instability further exacerbated tensions, while economic development remained stunted by the absence of basic infrastructure such as roads.

Gender inequality, too, loomed large, with women and girls facing barriers to accessing technology and education. Deep-rooted stereotypes perpetuated the belief that technology was the realm of men, depriving many of the opportunity to harness its potential.

Despite these formidable obstacles, hope flickered brightly on the horizon as the Akobo Youth Center played host to a momentous occasion. On May 28, 2022, the air buzzed with anticipation as parents, local authorities, and esteemed guests converged to celebrate the graduation of 16 resilient individuals. At this ceremony, there were 224 total attendees—the 16 graduates, and 208 parent, authorities, and colleagues that were invited.

In this remote corner of the world, where the odds were stacked against them, these graduates emerged as beacons of hope, illuminating the path towards a brighter future. Their achievements served as a testament to the transformative power of education and the indomitable spirit of the human soul.

One of the graduates of the Akobo Graduation was Minyong Bagot Kueth (pictured on the following pages holding one of his certificates); he received six certificates from the University of Virginia. Mr. Minyong Bagot Kueth took the following courses from the University of Virginia (UVA): Digital transformation; Design Thinking for Innovation; Customer Centric IT Strategies; Experiencing Design: Deepening your Design Thinking Practice; Digital Product Management; Fundamentals of Project Planning and Management.

Minyong Baguot Kueth's journey with DeAfrica began when financial constraints forced him to drop out of school after secondary education. With no funds and bleak prospects, he questioned how success could be achieved without college. DeAfrica became his answer. Through the Africa Scholarship Cohort, Minyong completed six courses and received six certificates, transforming his life, and proving that determination conquers adversity.

Above and below: students from the University of Bangui, Central African Republic Inaugural DeAfrica Graduation Ceremony, 2012

Students from the University of Bangui, Central African Republic
2012 DeAfrica Graduation

Graduates from the Akobo Graduation

Above and below: additional graduates from the Akobo Graduation.

Generosity of South Sudanese: a gift of a goat which could not be carried back to the US; a big party was organized, and the goat was cooked with rice and vegetables.

The Norwegian Refugee Compound: my room in Akobo—the challenge was the door which is extremely low for tall people like me. I had to bend or almost crawl in to get inside the room.

CHAPTER 9

A DIFFICULT JOURNEY

Since establishing DeAfrica in 2011 in Kenya, my journey has been one of relentless dedication. I've traversed the African continent by plane, bus, motorcycle, and even canoe, braving crocodile-infested rivers, rebel-occupied forests, and perilous bridges to spread the mission of my foundation far and wide.

Upon my return to Washington DC, after years of grappling with the challenges of launching DeAfrica due to funding constraints, a breakthrough moment arrived. I reached out to my former boss, Professor Peter Materu at the World Bank, seeking assistance for my nonprofit organization. Through his introduction, I had the privilege of meeting Professor Marito Garcia, who then guided me to the Darden School of Business at the University of Virginia.

In Washington DC, I adopt a frugal lifestyle, commuting to work by bicycle and utilizing the Metro system to conserve funds for my foundation's mission of aiding Africans.

As the Founder and President of Distance Education for Africa, Inc. (DeAfrica), a nonprofit organization committed to providing online courses across all 54 African nations, I am honored to have been recognized as one of the "Top 100 Most Influential People in Online Learning Africa." Education is my life's passion, driven by the belief that it holds the power to transform societies and foster prosperity.

A Daring Trip Across Three African Countries
Senegal → Guinea-Bissau → Guinea-Conakry → Senegal

Senegal: Dakar to Zinguinchore
I started this trip in Dakar, the capital city of Senegal. From Dakar, I took an inexpensive ferry boat from Dakar to Casamance. This is an

affordable means of transport to travel in Senegal with a starting price of 5000F cfa (around $10) per person if you are Senegalese or a resident. It is a very comfortable boat, and the trip is overnight. The boat leaves around 5pm and arrives in Zinguichore the next morning.

I spent one night in a small hotel in the city of Zinguichore, Senegal before taking a seven-seat Peugeot to travel to the capital of Guinea-Bissau. It wasn't a bad trip.

To Guinea-Bissau

I spent three days in Bissau, the capital of Guinea-Bissau. There, I went to the University of Amical Cabral to promote DeAfrica's programs at the computer science and the language departments. I was told that there was a shortage of infrastructure such as computer and challenges with the internet connection at the computer science department. I then continued my journey towards Guinea-Conakry.

For my trip from Bissau, I continued to Burutuma at the border between Guinea-Bissau and Guinea-Conakry. There, I crossed the border to go to Conakry, Guinea. I traveled through Bafatá, the second-largest city in Guinea-Bissau, all the way to Gabu.

When I finally reached Gabu, I found that I had missed the last public bus going toward Guinea-Conakry. I was told that I would have to wait for the next day to catch another public transport. Not wanting to wait until the next day, I asked what my other options were. I was told there was an alternate means of transport—motor-taxi. Some young men have become entrepreneurs by transporting people on their motorbikes; it is a niche way for young people to make money.

There were two major challenges with riding the motorbike.

The first challenge was that I had my large suitcase that usually had to be checked at airports. The suitcase was full of clothes for meetings (suits and ties) and DeAfrica materials. I asked how it would be possible to travel with the big suitcase on a motorbike and they told me that they do it all the time, showing me how it could be tied behind me. They nicely wrapped my suitcase in blue plastic in case of rain or when crossing rivers and off we went.

The second challenge was the sitting position—it was very uncomfortable. My back against the suitcase and the driver in front of me did not give me—at six feet tall—a lot of room for my long legs. I was squeezed during the entire 6–7-hour trip to Guinea-Conakry, literally grabbing my seat the entire trip.

During this trip, we went through forests, small villages, and over trails that only locals know very well. On some of the trails, branches would scratch my legs and arms. Crossing some small shallow rivers was the hardest part because I didn't know how deep they were, and my shoes and pants would get wet. The driver did not care, he was just going ahead, slowing down as we crossed some rivers. We were heading towards the Eastern part of the country, crossing the Gabu region. Senegal is located to the North and Guinea to the East and South of the Gabu region; the principal river, the Corubal River, flows through the region.

The Courbal River
The crossing of this river scared me to death because I don't know how to swim. If the canoe had flipped, I certainly would have drowned. I asked the canoe manager if there were crocodiles and he responded, 'Yes'. We crossed the river safely without any issues. We then continued through small trails known only to locals through the forest, going through Boé National Park.

Boé is a settlement located along the Courbal River in the southeastern Gabu Region of Guinea-Bissau and Boé National Park lies along the banks of the river. The park is famous for some endangered animal species, including the Western Chimpanzee, one of the four most endangered subspecies of chimpanzee. There are also baboons, vervets, patas, and Colobus monkeys in the park.

When we reached the border town of Burutumu, we had to stop at a checkpoint for customs. I had to open my suitcase, and everything had to be checked, the authorities searching for illegal substances.

Guinea-Conakry

Once past the checkpoint, we entered the territory of Guinea-Conakry, a French-speaking country. We reached a police checkpoint in the middle of nowhere. The *gendarmes*, or policemen, took the driver into their office; they were speaking a mix of mandingo, my mother's tongue, and French. This put me at ease because I understood both languages.

After the checkpoint, the driver took me to a small village and dropped me off at a hotel that he seemed to know very well; I'm sure he regularly brought customers there. He then returned to Guinea-Bissau. I could not sleep in the hotel with the mosquito bites and the heat. It was so hot that it felt like I was in an oven. I spent the whole night with my eyes opened, trying to kill the mosquitoes that were all over my body. I had done dangerous trips before in Africa, but this one was the most daring and dangerous.

The next day, I took another seven-seat Peugeot to cross the entire country—going from the northern part of Guinea all the way down to Conakry in the southern part of the country. I spent three days in Conakry. There, I went to the University Koffi Anan, a private university to make a presentation on DeAfrica and e-learning.

My final destination was completed there in Conakry, the capital of Guinea-Conakry. Now, I had to head back to Dakar, Senegal.

Return to Senegal

The return trip from Conaky to Dakar by car is also a breathtaking adventure. There are incredible landscapes and truly beautiful scenery.

The distance of the trip is 1311.6 kilometers and takes 18-20 hours by road and costs between $160-240 USD. There are dangerous bridges to be crossed, shown in pictures in this book where I am turning a chain to move our car and the bridge. This was a moving bridge; a bridge that is tied with chain that an operator turns with an iron bar to move the bridge.

We drove all day in a brand-new four-wheel car the first day, only taking some lunch breaks. We brought some fruit and cooked food along the way. The driver took some unpaved roads as shortcuts to speed up the trip. It took us almost two days to reach Dakar.

The Courbal River

Above and below: crossing the border from Guinea-Bissau to Guinea-Conakry (June, 2011)

Crossing the border from Guinea-Bissau to Guinea-Conakry

Going to Conakry, the Capital of Guinea

Winding up the chain of a moving bridge in Guinee on the way to Senegal

Crossing a dangerous bridge from Guinea to Senegal

Crossing a dangerous bridge from Guinea to Senegal

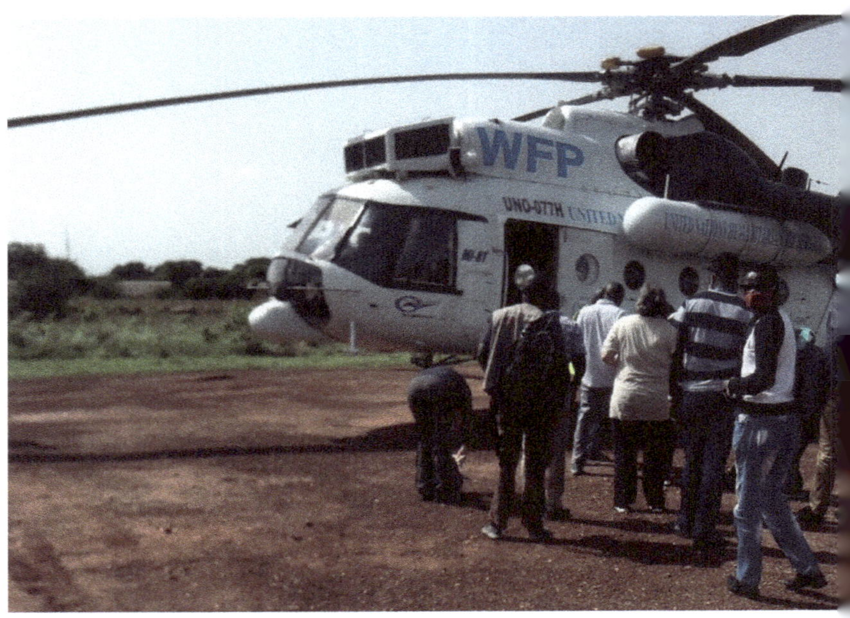

Travelling on a United Nations Helicopter from Juba to Akobo.

CHAPTER 10

STORIES OF GIVING BACK TO THE COMMUNITY

The individuals in the following pages are making a difference in their communities through their dedicated efforts to help others.

Oudou Bengaly
Mali

A Kenya Cyber Security Report released in June 2014 showed that Kenya was losing Sh5 billion every year to cyber fraud, and 2.1 billion was spirited out of financial institutions last year (Sunday Nation 11/16/2014). Because cyber-attacks were rampant all over Africa, DeAfrica offered some courses in cyber security to students and professionals in Africa in 2013 and 2014. Mr. Bengaly Oudou took DeAfrica course on cyber security called Advanced Persistent Threats (APT)-taught by Dr. Rose Shumba from the University of Maryland University College (UMUC).

After completing the course, Bengaly started a radio talk show to inform, warn, and sensitize the local populations and the police of his town called Sikasso in Mali about the dangers of cybercriminals. Mr. Bengaly Oudou managed to help an elderly woman who was about to be scammed and defrauded of 300,000 CFA francs (about $700) by a cybercriminal who had promised to help the son of the old woman enroll in a Canadian University. His talk shows benefited an entire community.

Rhoda Linlaat Machar

South Sudan

Rhoda defines the village of Akobo as an eye-opener, she believes in women establishments, Akobo as her field location gave her so many words to talk about, e.g., girl child education, a lot of women out there have vision that life didn't give them a chance. The traditional claim is the work of a woman is to sit home and give birth, but there is more to that; a woman who is educated is a pillar to the family, country, and a hope to the nation. Rhoda wants to break the traditional taboo and give women a chance to defend their true selves and become the answer to the universe.

Today she managed to educate two girl children this year. She believes it's never too late to build an empire for women structures and give them a chance to test life and believe in their dreams, e.g., to join education centers, doing business for themselves, and with the help of Distance Education for Africa (DeAfrica), Rhoda will continue to do more and create a Hub for women where they get to discuss their future dreams, desires, and plans for 2023. She will not only change the village of Akobo but she will extend it to more villages such as Urol and Walgak.

There is more and a bright future in these women who never got a chance to appreciate themselves. She believes it's her opportunity to make it work and be an answer to her generation. She will give hope to the hopeless and growing up with a lot on her shoulders when she was a little girl. She will transform women's lives and be the voice of the unspoken.

With the help of DeAfrica, she will contribute to extending the distance education learning to other locations, and she is glad there is a change in Akobo where women are participating, "as long as God wakes her up, it ain't over".

Boniswa Banyani
Botswana

Boniswa Banyani is a dream chaser, and her career is defined by the impact she makes in people's lives. Since completing the Project Planning course, she has been fortunate to be involved in various exciting projects. For instance, she is currently working on a creative art project involving a 9-meter, 3.3-ton robot statue called KAJUMO. Furthermore, she entered a creative business competition and was selected as one of the top 13 finalists nationwide.

She also had the privilege of assisting Matsieng Gardens in executing their first women's picnic, and she helped Lamp Serge host their first agricultural symposium in Lesotho. Moreover, she has been able to assist the various organizations she volunteers for in securing funding for their projects and proposals.

Her career has been marked by these successes, and the knowledge and skills she gained from the Project Planning course have been instrumental in these achievements. In her previous role as an Assistant Research Officer for a Member of Parliament's constituency office, the course helped her work more efficiently and effectively in serving the people and making a positive impact on their lives.

Saman Ange Michel Gougou
Cote d'Ivoire

Saman Ange Michel Gougou, from Cote d'Ivoire, a West Africa francophone country, is a lifelong learner scholar involved in research, digital communication, and English Language Teaching as a volunteer. As a servant leader, he is involved in various community services to share and empower others in a perspective of sustainable development and problem-solving including education for all.

His experience in Massive Open Online Courses (MOOCs) since 2015, taking Courses on Coursera through DeAfrica and University of Virginia, was a great opportunity to learn, share in communities, and change the world.

Angela Marufu
Tanzania

Angela Marufu from Tanzania has gone through a number of courses with Coursera, including Smart Growth for Small Business, and has benefited a lot.

She was involved with a social group of 40 women who are young graduates, and most of them are starting out in life. They are involved in activities aimed at empowering women in society. This season, one of their activities was that they agreed that educating women is empowering society. They have been asked to come up with business proposals for what business one wants to start then people will be put in groups, etc. She shared with them about the "SMART GROWTH FOR SMALL BUSINESS. She realized that it's very important to learn what to do about business right from the beginning instead of making mistakes first.

Louisia Irojioku
Botswana

Louisia Irojioku is making a difference in the future of youth. In 2019, as the future moves towards digitalization, she pursued the Digital Transformation Course on Coursera offered by the University of Virginia.

She expressed gratitude to Sidiki Traore and DeAfrica for the opportunity to do this course. It is helping her play her role as the current curator of the Global Shapers Gaborone Hub by bringing insight to help the Hub drive discussions as youths on how our future will be affected by digital transformations.

PART IV:

CONCLUSION & APPENDIX

CONCLUSION

In conclusion, my unwavering passion for education has catalyzed transformative change, impacting countless lives across the African continent.

Through dedicated efforts, we have cultivated the largest online community, fostering collaboration and support through platforms like WhatsApp, guided by the Community of Inquiry (CoI) framework. Lives have been irrevocably altered for the better, with individuals equipped with the skills and knowledge garnered from the African Scholarship Cohort now emerging as business strategists and consultants, poised to shape the future of our continent.

As we reflect on our journey, it's evident that our collective commitment to education has ushered in a new era of opportunity and empowerment, laying the groundwork for continued growth and prosperity across Africa.

NOTES

For this book, I used the following sources:

Duncan, Nancy Wadsworth. *The Nail That Sticks Up: An American Woman in Asia and Africa.* Paperback ed., 10 Sept. 2007.

"Somaliland Going Alone." *The Economist*, 17 Oct. 2015, p. 55.

The Economist. "Banking in Africa." *The Economist*, 17 Oct. 2015, p. 78.

Norwegian Refugee Council. "Building Peace Through Connectivity." *NRC.* www.nrc.no/shorthand/stories/building-peace-through-connectivity/index.html

Norwegian Refugee Council. "Breaking the Bias in South Sudan." *NRC.* www.nrc.no/shorthand/stories/breaking-the-bias-in-south-sudan/index.html

APPENDIX A: REACTIONS FROM COLLEAGUES TO MY DEPARTURE FROM THE AFRICAN VIRTUAL UNIVERSITY IN 2010

From: Sidiki Traore
To: staff
Cc: Bakary Diallo
Subject: Leaving the AVU in December 2010

Dear Colleagues

I will be leaving the AVU on December 31, 2010 after 12 years of helping build the AVU which is **now a well-respected institution**. I am extremely proud of a job well done.

My first position in Washington was that of ESL Program Coordinator. Since that time, I have worked continuously with AVU while undertaking new roles and broader responsibilities:

- initiated several projects and actions of benefit to AVU such as the compilation of AVU's registration and participation statistics, negotiation, and arrangement of cost-saving measures for AVU and pioneering the application of the new course fee policy that resulted in AVU's first revenue from sites in Africa (Université Lumiere from Bujumbura, Burundi was the first University to honor its financial obligation by sending fees to the Worldbank for the AVU

- worked tirelessly with students (to write petitions to the President of the Worldbank) and VCs to convince the Worlbank not to shut down the AVU in 1999 at the end of the Pilot Phase and to fund degree programs in Computer Science therefore we took the AVU from its darkest days to a better day today

- designed, developed, delivered many AVU Short courses in IT, Journalism, Language and professional seminars including JAVA REVOLUTION from MIT, one of the most

popular courses ever designed by the AVU. More than
200 students were able to get certificates from MIT for the
first time in their lives without leaving Africa

- worked with several content providers from around the
  World (USA, Canada, Belgium, Australia)

- participated in the design, implementation and the
  successful delivery of the Francophone Computer Science
  Degree to 9 francophone countries where about 290
  students were trained

- participated in the site evaluation missions for the
  Anglophone Computer Science that was offered to 9
  Anglophone countries

- participated in the facilitators training for the Francophone
  Computer Science, the Anglophone Computer Science,
  the Business Studies for Anglophone countries

- initiated fundraising campaign for Institutions in Somalia
  that landed on the Shernet Project; worked on and
  produced part of documents for the bidding of the UEMOA,
  participated in securing grant from Imperial Tobacco, that
  will be supporting the AVU for 6 years

- extended the AVU' network by opening over 45 Learning
  Centers across Africa,   including post conflict zones in
  Africa in Somalia (7 Universities on Somalia),
  Sudan, DRC(journalists from Goma, a small town in
  Eastern DRC, gained professional training for the first time
  in their lives)

- participated in the sensitization mission of ACEP in 9
  francophone Universities

- promoted, manned both, presented the AVU at
  International conferences in Washington DC, North Africa
  (Morocco, Algeria, Sudan) Indian Ocean (Mauritius,
  Seychelles, Madagascar),   Central Africa (Gabon, DRC,
  Cameroon), Southern Africa (Angola, Lesotho, South
  Africa) and West Africa (from Mauritania up to Benin.
  Visited 40 African countries in my 12 years with the AVU

- opened the West African Regional Office and made it operational (Host Country Agreement signed, bank accounts signed and so on)

- initiated the design of the Certificate in Renewable Energy, one of the most popular courses of the AVU, participated in the delivery, design and marketing of the Certificate in Renewable Energy

- participated in E-learning Africa to promote the AVU, built partnerships with different institutions (USAID-Kenya and so on)

- built strong partnerships with reputable institutions like the MIT' s project called LINC: Learning International Networks Consortium. Since its creation, I made sure that AVU never missed any meeting. The AVU has actively participated in the LINC meetings:

> Dr. Diarra in 2003
> Dr. Magdallen 2004
> Peter Bateman 2005
> Peter Dzvimbo in 2006
> Dr. Bakary Diallo 2007
> No Link in 2008
> Dr. Bakary Diallo in 2009
> Dr. Bakary Diallo in 2010

The list will be too long, but I wanted to share with few highlights of my achievements in building the AVU.

My last day with the AVU will be December 31st 2010. I have appreciated working with you. Best luck with the AVU.

Regards,

Sidiki Traore

--

Visit our website for more information: www.avu.org

From: Therrezinha Fernandes
To: Declan Ottaro; Catherine Wangeci K-Thuo; Sidiki Traore
Cc: Bakary Diallo; staff
Subject: RE : Leaving the AVU in December 2010

Dear Sidiki,

This a great list of some of your achievements, congratulations! You were and are still a great, if not the greatest, believer of the AVU since its inception and your optimism and faith in the future of the AVU always astonished me.

I want to thank you for all the support and advises and your kindness since my arrival at the Dakar office. It has been a pleasure meeting you and working with you. I will miss you.

I wish you all the best! Good Luck!

Kind regards, Tessa

À: Therrezinha Fernandes; Sidiki Traore
Objet : RE: Leaving the AVU in December 2010

Totally agreed Tessa. And all the best with the Dakar office too.
You must tell Sidiki to leave you with all the contacts of the immigration people so we can continue enjoying 'visa on entry' when we visit. It as always such a relief.

Best Regards,
Catherine

From: Therrezinha Fernandes
To: Sidiki Traore; Catherine Wangeci K-Thuo
Subject: RE : Leaving the AVU in December 2010

Catherine, as Loreal put so well, Sidiki worth it!!! :-)

Regards, Tessa

From: Catherine Wangeci K-Thuo
To: Therrezinha Fernandes
Cc: Sidiki Traore
Subject: RE: Leaving the AVU in December 2010

Tessa, this is a real nice message to Sidiki. Deservedly !!! Sidiki, we
shall miss you.

Best Regards,
Catherine

From: Catherine Wangeci K-Thuo
To: Sidiki Traore
Cc: Bakary Diallo; staff
Subject: RE: Leaving the AVU in December 2010

Dear Sidiki,

I wish you all the best in future endeavors.

You sure have made remarkable contribution in the growth of the AVU since inception and you shall go down in its history as one of the longest serving staff members.

Best Regards,
Catherine

De: Sidiki Traore
À: Catherine Wangeci K-Thuo; Therrezinha Fernandes
Objet : RE: Leaving the AVU in December 2010

Catherine
I am so touched and honored by all these kind words. I am leaving the AVU with a sense of JOB DONE. I could not make a list of all the achievements.

Sidiki Traore

From: James Wachira
To: Sidiki Traore
Cc: staff
Subject: RE: Leaving the AVU in December 2010

Dear Sidiki,

This is a great number of achievements you have been
able to accomplish while at the AVU.

We have appreciated working with you too.

Wishing you the best in your future endeavors.

Kind Regards,
James Wachira
ICT Assistant
--
www.avu.org

From: Marcella Magara
To: Sidiki Traore; staff
Cc: Bakary Diallo
Subject: RE: Leaving the AVU in December 2010

Dear Sidiki,

Your contribution to the AVU can't go unmentioned,
congratulations. It has been a great pleasure
working with you. I do appreciate your support, patience and
guidance.

May God bless you and your family in your future plans.

Good luck and all the best.

Best Regards,
Marcella.

From: Sidiki Traore
To: Marcella Magara; staff
Cc: Bakary Diallo
Subject: RE: Leaving the AVU in December 2010

Dear Marcella

Thanks lot. You and I have both contributed to helping this institution as well as other staff members. It was a great pleasure working with you.

Regards,

Sidiki Traore

From: Dinah Muthuka
To: Sidiki Traore; staff
Subject: RE: Leaving the AVU in December 2010

Dear Sidiki,
Wow. Definitely your impact to the AVU and across Africa will go into records.

I wish you all the best in your new chapter in life.

Kind regards
Ms. Dinah Muthuka.
Accountant

AVU Headquarters
The African Virtual University
Cape Office Park (Opposite Yaya Center)
Ring Road, Kilimani
Please click visit *www.avu.org*

From: Julius Abwao
To: Sidiki Traore; Marcella Magara; staff
Cc: Bakary Diallo
Subject: RE: Leaving the AVU in December 2010

It was a great pleasure working with you. Your contribution to helping this institution to where it has reached. I remember those old days which we used to work almost overnight making sure that AVU comes to the map.

God is to be with you in all ways.

Best regards,
Julius.

From: Sidiki Traore
To: staff
Subject: RE: Leaving the AVU in December 2010

Dear Julius

Thank you very. I am glad that you remember that I used to wake at 3:00 am in the morning to go to the studio in Washington DC and start the AVU courses at 6:00 am (Washington time) because of time difference.

The Women's Leadership seminar we broadcast live in Botswana was the longest ever (we started at midnight in Washington and finished the next day at 12 noon Washington time).

I am confident that Dr, Diallo and the team will carry on.

Thanks for your wishes.

Regards
Sidiki Traore

De: Declan Ottaro
À: Catherine Wangeci K-Thuo; Sidiki Traore
Cc: Bakary Diallo; staff
Objet : RE: Leaving the AVU in December 2010

Dear Sidiki,

In agreement with the sentiments made by my colleagues, it has
been an honor working with you.
The impact that you made at the AVU shall surely outlive you.

I wish you and your family the best in the next phase of your lives.

Regards,
Declan Ottaro
ICT Specialist I AfDB-AVU Multinational Support Project I African
Virtual University

APPENDIX B: MESSAGES FROM FORMER COLLEAGUES REGARDING MY AVU DEPARTURE

Benjamin Brett (former colleague)

Dear Sidiki,

You have indeed been the icon of AVU and stood by it from its inception to the respected giant it is at the moment.

I wish you and your family all the best as you embark on your next phase.

Kind regards,
B. Bett

Solomon Muthoka (former course moderator)

Dear Sidiki,

Thanks for your contribution. You have transformed education in Africa.

Wish you all the best and God blessing in your future endeavors.

Kind regards,
Solomon

Pauline Ngimwa (former colleague)

Mon Frere,

Don't tell me you are serious…you the last person who should leave the AVU!

Besides those great achievements which I know too well, I will always have fond memories of our time together especially sharing that big office during my first years at the AVU. You were great those days and that's why you will never stop being my dear and special frère.

I know its for very good reasons that you have left the AVU. John Fitzgerald Kennedy once said ***"Change is the law of life. And those who look only to the past or present are certain to miss the future".*** So I wish you the very best in the future as you move on to another phase in your life. Please keep me updated on your happenings, God bless you.

Ta soeur Pauline

P.S. - By the way I have gone through your list of achievements and been reminded of how you traversed the continent opening centres. Two of them are quite vivid because you brought me some gifts which I still treasure. When you went to DRC, you brought me a set of black jewellery (necklace and earrings) from a special stone. I lost the necklace but the earrings are a weekly wear, can you believe that? During one of your trips to Somalia, you brought me a red maroon scarf which I still keep in Kenya. Isn't that wonderful to be reminded of that great work you did not just for AVU but for our great continent! Am sure you will be remembered long after we have left this world God knows when that will be! I dream of going back to African HE, oh it was great fun enhancing ICT in education though there were those tearful moments.

Dear Sidiki,

It was wonderful and amazing how you supported the Somali Universities by implementing distance learning programs for ever and the first time in history.

1500 students benefited University of Hargeisa ODeL Center, you are one of our heroes and role models and
I hope while you are in New York you will continue by supporting and advising us to continue the
developments you have made.

Thank you, and wishing you good luck with your wife.

Regards,

Abdirashed Ibrahim Sh. Abdirahman
University of Hargiesa
Director, ICT Services & Distance Learning Department | UoH ACCA Exam Co-ordinator

University of Hargiesa (Somaliland)

Dear Sidiki,

Thank you very much for this. You know I value your interest and resilience in the pursuit of educational opportunities for the young of Africa.

Of course, I am very much interested.

Regards,
Hassan Heiss

Former ODEL Center Director, Puntland State University

Sidiki,
The world ever keeps appearing small. With your heart and great desire for making things happen, I just feel jealousy for those New Yorkers because they are going to get one of the best African sons ever. I could simply say, one day, you will be Kofi Annan's league. Bravo and keep the flag flying.

God bless you and have the best of times. Leave your lines open, I will always keep you in my focus and a target of inspiration.

Norman

Puntland State University, Garowe

Dear Sidiki
We are very much appreciating you smooth collaboration and cooperation during our partners.We hope good prosperity where ever you are.

Mohamud Hamid Mohamed
Kaalo Relief & Development Director and Puntland State
University President
Garowe, Puntland State of Somalia

Université Cheick Anta Diop (Dakar, Senegal)

Un vieux Mohican quitte l'UVA après avoir conduit la résistance victorieuse à tous les assauts.

Nous étions là ensemble aux toutes premières attaques. Ces douze années seront marquées d'une
touche blanche.

Bon vent, Big Man!
Pr A. camara

Université de Ouagadougou (Burkina-Faso)

Bonsoir

Je te remercie grandement de partager avec nous tous, ce bilan que je sais non exhaustif, pour avoir été parmi les tous premiers à rejoindre ce processus en 1997 après la conférence de l'UVA Dakar.

A tous de tenir haut le flambeau que tu as si dignement transmis.

Tu as été la pièce maitresse, la cheville ouvrière de cette grande entreprise qu'a été l'UVA avec ses succès et ses échecs.

Tous mes veux de bonheur t'accompagne auprès de ta famille et aux USA que tu as quitte 12 ans durant pour servir la jeunesse africaine.

Du courage et bonne route, mon frère.

Hamidou TOURE
Professeur
Université de Ouagadougou

Université de Ouagadougou (Burkina-Faso)

Bonjour Sidiki,
Ce n'est pas sans émotion que je prends connaissance de ton départ de l'UVA, un bébé pour qui tu as tant donné! Que tu en sois ici remercié.

Je joins donc ma voix à la celle de notre communauté pour te dire encore une fois merci pour tout ce qui as fait et te souhaite bon vent pour tes activités futures.

A bientôt sur d'autres fronts

=====
Oumarou SIE
Université de Ouagadougou

Université Cheick Anta Diop (Dakar, Senegal)

Je ne sais pas quoi dire! Je sais que nous avons tous des obligations mais certaines séparations sont toujours difficiles. Que Dieu vous accompagne! L'UVA a bcp contribué au système éducatif. Nous prions pour un rayonnement encore pendant des années. Merci pour tout. Les résultats de la phase pilote commencent à sortir dans la plateforme http://www.fastef-fad.org/ . Je pense que vous allez assister à la cérémonie de remise des diplômes qui sera fixée très prochainement.
Merci encore
Dr. Ibrahim Cissé

Université de Bamako (Mali)

Bonjour,
je te remercie beaucoup pour le service que tu as rendu à mon pays à travers l'UVA. Tu as travaillé sans relâche pour le Mali.
Je prie le BON DIEU de te récompensera pour ton esprit ouvert, ta collaboration franche et attachement au travail bien fait.
Merci mon fils mes bénédictions t'accompagnent.
Dogo Moussa KONE
CEUVA Bamako Mali.

Université de Douala (Cameroun)

Bjour Sidiki,

Au moment où vous quittez l'UVA après tout ce que vous avez fait pour qui sommes de cette communauté. Que le Dieu Puissant vous protège et vous ouvre grandement les portes où vous allez rejoindre votre famille.

Bon vent Grand Homme.

Salomé MOUTHE / Université de Douala
Centre UVA

Dear Sidiki,
As I use to say, it is always very sad every time we have to see one of our great family leaving for another professional adventure, particularly when the departure concerns one of the pioneers of the AVU in Africa.

I will always remember your name every time I think about the very beginning of the AVU, when the way was not as clear as it now. I will always remember your valuable contributions every time we needed to think about the best strategies to grow our business and to sustain the Centres in Africa.

You have really contributed to sustain the UVA Dakar you have seen it born and you have done your best to keep it active and sometime in very difficult local contexts. Your name will remain in the history of AVU forever.

AVU and the PRECA/VISAF/PILAF family will always remember your positiveness and your wish to see good thinks happening within the network as our contribution to the development and strengthening of capacities in Africa.

Everywhere you will be, for sure you will continue to work for your country and for Africa.

On behalf of BENIN AVU Center /AVU and on my own behalf, I want to wish you lots of success and happiness in your new commitment. We do hope to remain in touch and to continue to exchange views and ideas for particularly the development of the AVU in Africa and the development of Africa in general.

All the best and God bless you and your family

Jacques T. EDJROKINTO
Directeur du Centre d'Education à Distance du BENIN

Université de Nouakchott (Mauritanie)

Bonjour Sidiki,
A mon tour je ne peux qu'être très attristé par la nouvelle mais la vie continue et continuera sans nul doute vers de nouveaux horizons.

Je garde de très bon souvenir des efforts que tu as su apporter à la famille de l'UVA.Ton apport à l'UVA restera à tout jamais dans l'histoire de la formation FOAD en Afrique car parmi les initiateurs du programme à ces débuts (1997).

Gardons au moins le contact virtuellement dans le cas où nous n'aurons pas l'occasion de le faire en présentiel.

Merci encore une fois

Issa

Université de Saint Louis (Senegal)

My dear friend Sidiki,

It has been a real *plaisir* and an honor to work with you all these years. Your departure will leave a gap that will be difficult to fill. However being with your family is also important. For now you must know that the UVA staff in Saint Louis is sadden by the news.

We wish you a very happy life with your family and we want you to know also that you have a family in Saint Louis. We will be at your disposal should you need our assistance in your future life.

Have a merry Christmas and a happy New Year in New York with your family.

Take good care of yourself.
A. Barry

FASTEF (Dakar, Senegal)

Une grande surprise, empreinte d'émotion.

Que le Bon Dieu vous garde et vous donne longue vie, bonheur et prospérité auprès de votre famille et dans votre avenir
Ωprofessionnely Youssou Diop
Formateur TICE

FASTEF (Dakar, Senegal)

Bonjour Mr TRAORE!

Merci de l'information! Tout le plaisir a été pour moi de travailler avec vous. Je vous souhaite un bon retour auprès de votre famille. Je souhaite pouvoir vous rencontrer à d'autres occasions. Au revoir!

Mamdi Biaye
L'Assesseur de la FASTEF

ESIBA (Lome, Togo)

Cher ami Sidiki Traoré,

Permets-moi de te tutoyer pour te remercier de tes efforts pour une mise enyoeuvre enrichissante du partenariat entre l' UVA et l''ESIBA. Je garde de toi un excellent souvenir.

J'espère recevoir de tes nouvelles lorsque tu auras repris service aux USA.

Puisse, avec l'Amour de Dieu, l'année nouvelle 2011 être heureuse pour toi et pour tous ceux qui te sont chers !

A nous revoir.
Vovomé A. KUEVIAKOE

Université de Douala (Cameroun)

Tu as été le précurseur de ce magnifique chapitre ô combien riche et noble qui a fait du virtuel une réalité vraie, palpable et vécue en Afrique: l'UVA.

Je n'oublierai à aucun moment de ma vie cette magnifique expérience vécue à tes côtés, j'ai beaucoup appris pour ma faire valoir à ce jour toujours grâce à Toi plus particulièrement très cher Ami et Grand Frère SIDIKI et l'UVA en général promu à cette superbe "Bourse de l'UVA" du CIESA/CANADA, que je vis à merveille.

Je confirme mon expertise avec cet important diplôme du DESS-GME que je suis entrain d'obtenir en ce moment. Merci beaucoup et mille fois Merci!!!!!!!

J'ose croire tout simplement que ta nouvelle Vie aux "States" t'ouvrira grandement de nouvelles portes pour toi et ta famille avec "Grand Frère et Ami" et c'est de tout coeur que je te le souhaite, alors beaucoup de bonheur sur ton nouveau chemin et restons en contact permanents, et si je peux t'être utile au sortir de cet important Cursus du CIESA/CANADA, je ne manqeurai pas de retravailler encore avec Toi cette fois-ci "bardé" d'expériences fiables et confirmées. donne-moi seulement ton nouveau courriel si ça te dis, quant à moi je te dis tout simplement "MERCI" et bonne route.
Marcel Guillaume MOUTOME ton ami de toujours........

Bonjour Marcel Je te remercie beaucoup de ces mots qui sont allés droit au cœur. Je garderai mon email de Gmail et tu pourras toujours me contacter. Si jamais tu es a New York, fais moi signe pour que ma famille et moi te rencontre. Merci une fois. Sidiki Traore

---

Jamais je ne l'oublierai dans ma VIE car la reconnaissance et la gratitude ne sont que du domaine des êtres HUMAINS que nous et nous rendent véritablement HUMAINS, par rapport à une éventuelle rencontre physique à NEW YORK où ailleurs, il ne me reste qu'à joindre les deux mains et de faire appel aux Divinités du Ciel et de la Lune pour qu'elles agissent donc maintenant,

et çà va se faire, je reste convaincu car mon esprit est de voir
"Grand maintenant et ceci de plus en plus" car je peux déjà servir
partout grâce à l'expertise acquise auprès de la grande équipe de
l'UVA et du Centre UVA- Université de Douala -Cameroun
pourquoi pas!

Merci encore pour tout.
Marcel Guillaume MOUTOME

Université Abdou Moumouni (Niamey, Niger)

Bonjour Sidiki,

je viens juste de lire ta correspondance concernant ton
départ de l'UVA et suis très émus comme tous ceux qui ont
travaillé avec toi dans le cadre du projet UVA. Depuis mon
arrivée au Centre UVA de Niamey en 2005, j'ai toujours
hautement apprécié ton engagement pour les idéaux de
l'UVA. Personne n'oubliera à Niamey ta contribution
permanente à la réussite des différents programmes de
l'UVA: Bus. Communication, Cross-roads café, Academic and
business English et surtout les programmes de Laval - les
formations de courtes durées et le programme diplômant.
Au nom de toutes les personnes qui ont bénéficié des
services de l'UVA au Niger je te remercie vivement pour ta
contribution au développement de l'enseignement à
distance en Afrique. Je te souhaite plein succès aux USA et
pourquoi par encore en Afrique. Merci et merci. Du courage
Grand Frère Sidiki,

Bonne Chance - Tous mes voeux de santé et de prospérité
pour la nouvelle et la nouvelle étape de la vie.

Ousmane Manga Adamou
Directeur du Centre UVA de Niamey

Ecole Normale Supérieure (Dakar, Senegal)

Bonjour M. Traoré,

Nous avons eu le plaisir de travailler avec vous, votre présence a été nécessaire et utile pour la bonne continuation des activité de l'UVA, en tout cas, ce mon constat depuis le début de ma collaboration avec l'UVA à travers votre honorable présence et celle de Tessa,

Nous vous souhaitons un bon séjour avec votre famille à New York
Cordialement

Boudy Bilal
Faculté des Sciences et Technologies de l' Education et de la Formation
Universite Cheick Anta Diop

IMPACT Productions SUARL (Senegal)

Bonsoir Sidiki,
Je vous souhaite un bon retour aux USA et profitez bien de votre chère famille. Quant à nous, on garde le contact et c'est un réel plaisir de vous avoir connu et côtoyé.

Bonnes fêtes et joyeux noël.

A très bientôt.

Amitiés,

Daniel
IMPACT Productions SUARL
SIADE Sénégal SARL

Ecole Supérieure Polytechnique (Dakar, Senegal)

bonjour Sidiki,
ce n'est pas une très bonne nouvelle, mais hélas dans toute
aventure, il ya une fin. ce fut très agréable de collaborer avec
vous. On garde le contact.
Plein de succès dans tes nouvelles activités

bien cordialement
Fadel

Dr Cheikh Mouhamed Fadel KEBE
Centre International de Formation et de Recherche en Énergie
Solaire
Ecole Supérieure Polytechnique

Papa Alioune Ndiaye (former colleague)

Bonjour Sidiki
J'ai beaucoup apprécié d' avoir collaboré avec toi au cours de ces
dernières années. J'ai aussi noté ton sens élevé des relations
humaines. C'est donc avec regret que j'apprends ton départ.
Bonne chance pour la suite et sois assuré de ma disponibilité pour
toujours collaborer avec toi.

Papa Alioune Ndiaye

"Le Soleil" Newspaper (Senegal)

Merci de cette marque de confiance mais j'espère que tu reviendras à
Dakar avant de repartir. En tout cas, je te remercie pour la collaboration
et du travail accompli. Que le Tout-Puissant guide encore tes pas et te
préserve des envieux.
Daouda Mané
Soleil, Sénégal

TreffpunkSenegal Allemagne-Mimbar
(Dakar, Senegal)

bonjour m. traoré,
Nous avons été brièvement en relation, mais nous avons eu à
apprécier votre disponibilité et votre générosité. Nous vous
souhaitons un plein succès aux usa et nous vous souhaitons une
bonne et heureuse année 2011
alassane diagne
M.ALASSANE DIAGNE
TREFFPUNKTSENEGAL ALLEMAGNE-MIMBAR

Simon Meledje (Journalist, Senegal)

MON TRES CHER EN ESPERANT QUE CE N EST QU UN
AUREVOIR JE TE SOUHAITE PLEIN SUCCES DANS TES
NOUVELLES FONCTION ,VRAIMENT CE FUT UNE
COLLABORATION SINCERE ET FRUCTUEUSE
MA FAMILLE SE JOIND A MOI EGALEMENT

BONNE ET HEUREUSE ANNEE
SIMON

Université Cheick Anta Diop (Dakar, Senegal)

Bonjour M. Sidiki Merci pour tout. cela a été un plaisir de travailler
avec vous. Bonne et heureuse année 2011.
Ibrahima NIANG

Université Cheick Anta Diop (Dakar, Senegal)

Cher Sidiki
Toutes séparations sont douloureuses mais nous vous souhaitons
une bonne vie aux USA.
Pr. Ibra DIENE

Bonjour Sidiki,
Douze années, c'est beaucoup et pas assez en même temps. Tout dépend des objectifs qu'on s'était assignés au départ. En tout état de cause, l'essentiel, c'est d'avoir rempli correctement sa mission. A mon humble avis, tout porte à croire que pour toi, cela a été le cas. Je voudrais donc saisir cette opportunité pour me permettre de te remercier, du fond du cœur, de la collaboration que tu as entretenue avec ma modeste personne, la FASTEF et l'UCAD et que j'ai trouvée efficace et empreinte d'humilité.

Je forme les vœux les meilleurs de te voir retrouver ta famille aux USA dans la joie et la prospérité.

Bonnes fêtes de fin d'année et au plaisir de nos futures retrouvailles.

∘∘

Igen Alioune Moustapha DIOUF
Enseignant-chercheur à la Fastef

∘∘

Université Cheick Anta Diop (Dakar, Senegal)

Bonjour, SIDIKI
Je viens d'apprendre ton départ de l'UVA. Il suscite en moi, à la fois, un sentiment de plaisir mêlé de nostalgie. Plaisir parce que je suis content de savoir que tu vas retrouver ta famille à New York. Nostalgie, parce que, pendant toutes ces années que tu as passées à l'UVA, non seulement nous avons noué des relations professionnelles qui ont permis à l'UCAD et à l'UVA de collabore de manière très efficace mais, en plus, nous avons eu des relations personnelles de très bon aloi. Pour toutes ces raisons, je te remercie et te dis toute ma disponibilité pour rester en contact avec toi. Bonne et heureuse année 2011 à toi et à toute ta famille. SALUTATIONS TRES CORDIALES.
M. Abdou Karim NDOYE

Université Cheick Anta Diop (Dakar, Senegal)

Bonjour Sidiki,
Merci de partager l'information. Bonne chance pour ton futur.
J'en profite pour te présenter mes meilleurs voeux de bonne et
heureuse année 2011.
Cordialement
--
Pr. Issakha YOUM
Département de Physique, Faculté des Sciences et techniques
Université Cheikh Anta DIOP de Dakar

Université de Kinsahsa
(Kinshasa, Democratic Republic of the Congo)

Merci beaucoup. Votre expertise acquise tout au long de
nombreuses années passées dans des institutions de formations à
distance est reconnue de tous. Nous allons continuer à compter
sur vous pour de nouvelles expériences dans ce vaste pays où les
besoins en formation vont croissant.
Bien cordialement.
Prof. Pierre MUKENDI WA MPOYI
Université de Kinshasa

Agence Sénégalaise pour les Energies Renouvables
(Senegal)

Mr Traoré,
Bonjour,
Nous te regretterons beaucoup surtout nous avons juste
commencé à collaborer Nous te souhaitons bon retour auprès de
la famille et bonne chance et pleins succès pour les actions
futures.
Cheikh Wade
CIER/ASER

Cher Sidiki,

Les mouvements sont le propre de la vie. Nous nous sommes rencontrés au cours de celle-ci dans le projet de l'UVA. Je voudrais témoigner de votre rôle très décisif pour les centres d'enseignements (CE) de l'UVA. Depuis Washington, au départ, nous nous avez aidé (centre de Saint-Louis) à configurer le satellite avec succès et à accéder aux premiers cours JAVA et anglais (Crossroad café).

Une fois à Nairobi, Vous et Madame Savard, avez été nos partenaires de choix pour lancer définitivement notre centre. Vous étiez aussi là au lancement du programme majeur du Bachelor en Sciences de l'Informatique. Je retiens de vous votre grande pédagogie. Devant les difficultés, votre optimiste nous a tous aidé passer les gués.

L'Afrique vous doit beaucoup puisque je considère que l'UVA est une belle réalisation panafricaine rendue possible grâce à des hommes comme vous et notre fidèle disparu Albéric Chimon. Nous pourrions vous rendre en perpétuant dans nos universités ces entres d'enseignements à distances en vue de relever le défi de remonter le TBS africain.

A Saint-Louis, l'Institut de Formations Ouvertes et à Distance (IFOAD) que j'avais lancé à mon départ, est maintenant une réalité sur le papier avec la signature du decrét. Soyez en honorés.

Cher ami, restons en contact car votre porte-feuille de contacts est énorme et nous ne manquerons pas de l'utiliser.

Gane Samb Lo
Ancien Directeur du CE UVA de l'UGB.

Hello my friend,

I'm very happy to read you to day. It's true, it's a long time tu m'as confié à Tessa, and she did her best to help me. L'UVA m'a fait confiance et j'essaye de le mériter. we hope to do our best pour te prouver que ton long soutien ne serra pas vain. I great you. Tu te souviens sans doute de nos débats passionnants à propos de la renaissance des noirs. C'était à Dakar. Il ne s'agissait pas pour nous d'une renaissance folklorique ou des choses de musée, qu'on va de temps en temps voir comme au cinéma. Il s'agissait d'un comportement de tous les jours pour sauvegarder, dans une vision innovante, nos valeurs culturelles et morales, d'une part et mais surtout de prouver notre grande capacité de comprendre et d'accepter la différence qui tous ensemble sont une beauté et un amour à même d'envelopper le développement humain durable de l'humanité.

Les noirs seront les plus nombreux et sans doute les plus forts dans les millénaires à venir. Il faut préparer cela dès maintenant pour qu'à notre ère, le monde soit plus humain, plus tolérant, plus solidaire, plus généreux dans une multiculture mondiale de respect de l'autre, de paix, d'abondance et de bonheur. J'espère qu'avant ma mort, à notre tour, je verrai des Etats et des Peuples noirs courir partout dans le monde pour apporter leurs contributions aux différents maux humains et naturels.

Bref! je ne vais pas recommencer comme si on est face à face à Dakar. Mais rappelles toi que je crois fermement à notre capacité de nous organiser dès maintenant pour ces nobles objectifs. Je travaille à me greffer ou à créer une fondation pour cela. Quand tu peux ou si tu en voies des opportunités dans cette vision, je suis là. C'est dans ce travail que je m'épanouirai le plus, alors aide moi à être heureux.

Il faut revenir à notre pain quotidien, n'est ce pas? Je souhaite que tu aies eu un meilleur poste aux USA pour mieux t'épanouir. Et, par la même occasion, je te souhaite mes vœux les meilleurs pour l'année 2011.Dégageons plus de temps pour nous écrire à l'avenir. Je me sauve.

Take care and my best regards to your familly.
LEOSSOGO Pascal.

Notre Dame de Tendresse (former colleague)

Merci Sidiki mais c'est dommage
Je vous souhaite bonne continuation pour la suite des travaux qui vous
sera confié

Soeur Odette

Indiana University of Pennsylvania (USA)

Wow ! That was great, Sidiki. Your name is deservedly ingrained in
AVU history. Congratulations for a job so perfectly and
professionally well done!

Best wishes

Stanford G. Mukasa, Ph.D.
Associate Professor
Journalism Department
Indiana University of Pennsylvania

ECOBANK (Dakar, Senegal)

Bonjour Mr Traore,

C'est fût un réel plaisir de vous avoir rencontré.
Bonne chance dans votre nouvelle vie. J'espère que nous nous
reverrons très bientôt.

Joyeuses fêtes et prenez bien soin de vous.

Regards,
Ndeye Penda DIOP
SOURANG
CORPORATE BANKING
ECOBANK, DAKAR